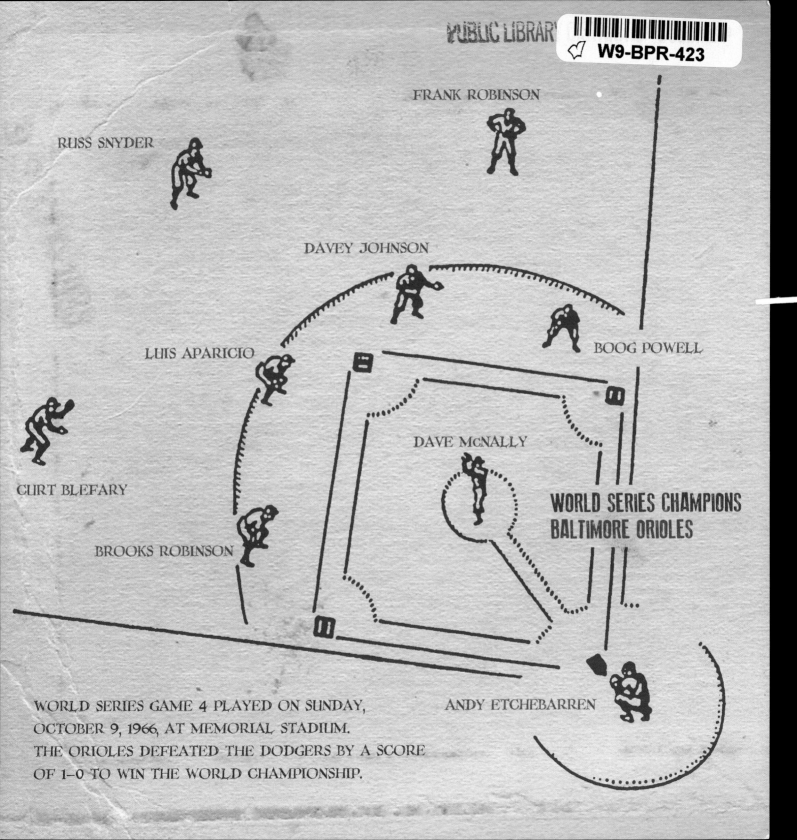

FRANK ROBINSON

RUSS SNYDER

DAVEY JOHNSON

LUIS APARICIO

BOOG POWELL

CURT BLEFARY

DAVE McNALLY

WORLD SERIES CHAMPIONS
BALTIMORE ORIOLES

BROOKS ROBINSON

ANDY ETCHEBARREN

WORLD SERIES GAME 4 PLAYED ON SUNDAY,
OCTOBER 9, 1966, AT MEMORIAL STADIUM.
THE ORIOLES DEFEATED THE DODGERS BY A SCORE
OF 1–0 TO WIN THE WORLD CHAMPIONSHIP.

WORLD SERIES CHAMPIONS

BALTIMORE ORIOLES

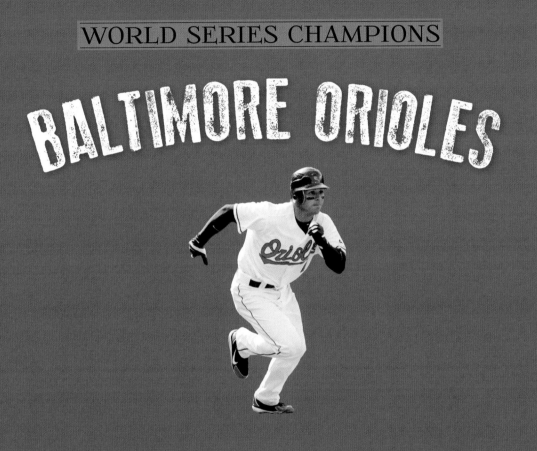

SARA GILBERT

CREATIVE
PAPERBACKS

Published by Creative Paperbacks
P.O. Box 227, Mankato, Minnesota 56002
Creative Paperbacks is an imprint of The Creative Company
www.thecreativecompany.us

Design and production by Blue Design (www.bluedes.com)
Art direction by Rita Marshall
Printed in the United States of America

Photographs by Corbis (Bettmann), Getty Images (Lisa Blumenfeld,
Linda Cataffo/NY Daily News Archive, Diamond Images, Jerry
Driendl, G. Fiume, Focus on Sport, Bob Gomel/Time & Life
Pictures, John Grieshop/MLB Photos, Harry How, Brad Mangin/
MLB Photos, Hunter Martin, Ted Mathias/AFP, J. Meric, Ronald
C. Modra/Sports Imagery, Hy Peskin/Time & Life Pictures,
Photofile/MLB Photos, Rich Pilling/MLB Photos, Jamie Squire,
Perry Thorsvik, Tony Tomsic/MLB Photos, Peter Stackpole/Time &
Life Pictures, Tim Umphrey, Dilip Vishwanat, Hank Walker/Time
& Life Pictures)

Library of Congress Cataloging-in-Publication Data
Gilbert, Sara.
Baltimore Orioles / Sara Gilbert.
p. cm. — (World series champions)
Includes bibliographical references and index.
Summary: A simple introduction to the Baltimore Orioles major
league baseball team, including its start in 1902 as the St. Louis
Browns, its World Series triumphs, and its stars throughout the
years.
ISBN 978-1-60818-259-6 (hardcover)
ISBN 978-0-89812-810-9 (pbk)
1. Baltimore Orioles (Baseball team)—History—Juvenile literature.
I. Title.
GV875.B2G54 2013
796.357'64097526—dc23   2011051186

First edition
9 8 7 6 5 4 3 2 1

Cover: Right fielder Nick Markakis
Page 2: Right fielder Frank Robinson
Page 3: Second baseman Brian Roberts
Right: Left fielder Gene Woodling

MIKE CUELLAR

LUKE SCOTT

BRIAN MATUSZ

RAFAEL PALMEIRO

DOUG DeCINCES

RON HANSEN

TABLE OF CONTENTS

BALTIMORE AND ORIOLE PARK

Baltimore is a **PORT** city in Maryland. Huge ships pass through its **HARBOR**. On summer nights, people on those ships can see the lights of Oriole Park at Camden Yards. A baseball team called the Orioles plays there.

RIVALS AND COLORS

The Orioles play major league baseball. All the major-league teams try to win the World Series to become world champions. Baltimore's uniforms are black and orange. The Orioles are **RIVALS** of the New York Yankees and Boston Red Sox.

SHORTSTOP CAL RIPKEN JR.

1970 WORLD SERIES

ORIOLES HISTORY

The Orioles' first season was in 1901. They played in Milwaukee, Wisconsin, for one year. Then they moved to St. Louis, Missouri, where they were called the Browns. During 52 years in St. Louis, the Browns got to the World Series once. But they lost.

1945 ST. LOUIS BROWNS

SS
MIGUEL TEJADA

RF
PAUL BLAIR

LF
JOHN LOWENSTEIN

2B
DAVEY JOHNSON

CF
AL BUMBRY

1B
BOOG POWELL

FRANK ROBINSON

In 1954, the Browns moved to Baltimore. They were renamed the Orioles. Soon, they became world champions. In 1966, outfielder Frank Robinson led the **UNDERDOG** Orioles to the World Series. Baltimore beat the Los Angeles Dodgers to win the championship!

JIM PALMER

Smart manager Earl Weaver helped the Orioles get to the World Series four times from 1969 to 1979. In 1970, the Orioles won their second championship.

The Orioles won another World Series in 1983. Star pitcher Jim Palmer helped Baltimore beat the Philadelphia Phillies. But the Orioles were not very good for the next 20 years.

EARL WEAVER

BROOKS ROBINSON

EDDIE MURRAY

ORIOLES STARS

Third baseman Brooks Robinson was 18 years old when he started playing for the Orioles in 1955. He won 16 Gold Glove awards for his great defense. In 1977, first baseman Eddie Murray began hitting homers in Baltimore. He hit more than 500 in his **CAREER**.

Starting in 1982, shortstop Cal Ripken Jr. played in 2,632 straight games for the Orioles. People called him the "Iron Man"! Ripken played many years with pitcher Mike Mussina. Mussina set **RECORDS** in Baltimore for strikeouts.

In 2006, right fielder Nick Markakis joined the Orioles. He helped Baltimore score many runs. His solid hitting helped fans believe that Baltimore could get back to the World Series soon!

MIKE MUSSINA

NICK MARKAKIS

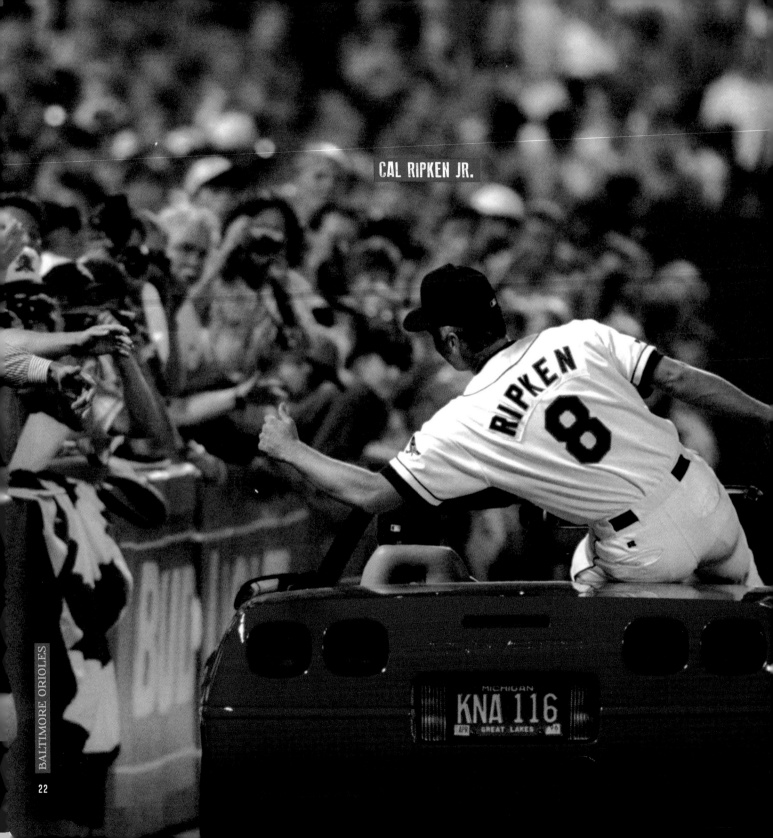

CAL RIPKEN JR.

HOW THE ORIOLES GOT THEIR NAME

The Orioles are named for beautiful orange-and-black birds. The Oriole is the official state bird of Maryland. Two earlier baseball teams in Baltimore were also named the Orioles. Fans sometimes call the Orioles the "O's" or "Birds."

ABOUT THE ORIOLES

First season: 1901

League/division: American League, East Division

World Series championships:

1966   4 games to 0 versus Los Angeles Dodgers

1970   4 games to 1 versus Cincinnati Reds

1983   4 games to 1 versus Philadelphia Phillies

Orioles Web site for kids:

http://mlb.mlb.com/mlb/kids/index.jsp?c_id=bal

Club MLB:

http://web.clubmlb.com/index.html

GLOSSARY

CAREER — all the years a person spends doing a certain job

HARBOR — a place for boats to stop

PORT — a town where ships are loaded and unloaded

RECORDS — performances that are the best ever

RIVALS — teams that play extra hard against each other

UNDERDOG — a person or team that is not expected to win

INDEX